Find It Now!

Proven Tips, Tricks & Strategies For Finding Practically <u>Anything</u> Online...Fast!

By Gilles Côté

© Copyright 2014 Gilles Côté

ALL RIGHTS RESERVED

No part of this book may be reproduced or transmitted in any form whatsoever, electronic, or mechanical, including photocopying, recording, or by any informational storage or retrieval system without express written, dated and signed permission from the author.

DISCLAIMER AND/OR LEGAL NOTICES:

The information presented herein represents the view of the author as of the date of publication. Because of the rate with which conditions change, the author reserves the right to alter and update his opinion based on the new conditions. This book is for informational purposes only. While every attempt has been made to verify the information provided in this book, neither the author nor his affiliates/partners assume any responsibility for errors, inaccuracies or omissions. Any slights of people or organizations are unintentional. If advice concerning legal or related matters is needed, the services of a fully qualified professional should be sought. This book is not intended for use as a source of legal, medical or financial advice.

Dedication

This book is dedicated to my wonderful wife Tracey who has supported me throughout the years through good times and bad and my two precious daughters Kayla and Emily who have taught me the power of unconditional love.

Table of Contents

INTRODUCTION 9

SEARCH ENGINES 101 11

HOW TO BECOME A SEARCH NINJA 15

BECOME AN EXPLORER 25

MORE TIPS THAT YOU CAN HANDLE 27

RELATED SEARCHES 29

LIGHTNING SPEED RESULTS 33

GOOGLE DEEP DIVE 35

NEWS THAT MATTERS TO YOU 37

GO TREASURE HUNTING 41

SITE SEARCH SECRETS 45

I WANT ANSWERS! 49

CROWDSOURCED ENCYCLOPEDIA 55

'HOW TO' NIRVANA 57

CONTENT POWERHOUSE 59

HOW DOES THAT WORK? 61

FINE-TUNE YOUR LIFE 63

LIFE HACKS 65

BARGAINS FROM MISSPELLINGS 67

AMAZON UNADVERTISED DEALS 69

BUY GIFTS BASED ON PERSONALITY 71

SHOP THE WORLD 73

SAVE SOME HEADACHES 75

PRODUCT SUPPORT MADE EASY 77

HOW TO REPLACE BOOKS 79

HOW TO REPLACE MAGAZINES 81

HOW TO BECOME A POWER SHOPPER 83

VIDEO SEARCH POWER 87

IMAGE SEARCH POWER 89

MAP SEARCH POWER 93

REPLACE PAID SOFTWARE 95

TIME SAVERS 97

WILDCARD 99

RESOURCES 101

ABOUT THE AUTHOR 102

Introduction

Searching still remains one of the most popular activities online. Why?

Because there's always a need for more information...whether it's for work, home or just for play, we have an insatiable hunger for information!

People, places, hobbies, events, companies, products, music, TV, movies, books, food, homes, cars, pets, news, money, how-to's... you get the idea.

Information is the hot commodity of today, and you can start tapping into this goldmine online.

How are your current search skills? Can you easily find all the 'golden nuggets' out there waiting for you? Do you just go to Google, type in a couple of words, click the Search button and hope for the best? If this simple search query makes up more than 50% of your searches, you're missing out on so much 'gold' online, it will surprise you. You are just scraping the surface of what is available to you.

I love searching and especially finding stuff online. I have a passion for it. I'm not sure what it is about it, but I get a rush exploring and discovering the 'hidden' nuggets of information on the Internet.

Because of this, I'm familiar with a lot of online search resources, what they can do, and the various tips and tricks that can be used to pump every last drop of useful content from the Web.

The tips, tricks and strategies I am going to share in this book will not only help you to find practically anything you want online fast, but also improve your life in every way!

How? Well, having the ability to find solutions to everyday problems whether they are health, family, financial, work or anything else for that matter will give you the tools to cope or even overcome whatever challenges you may face.

It's time to become a search genius and uncover a whole new world of information that is literally at your fingertips.

Enjoy!

Search Engines 101

*Y*ou may not know it, but there are literally dozens if not hundreds of Internet search engines available.

No point wasting your time, so I'll focus on the best (in my humble opinion).

Google.com

An obvious choice but it is definitely worth mentioning because you're most likely not using its full potential and to be completely honest, it is my tool of choice for 95% of my searches so if you notice a bias for Google, it's because there is ☺. Here are just a few of the features that make it so powerful:

- **Relevancy** – You'll have a hard time finding a search engine that gets you the information/content/answers you're looking for better than Google. Other search engines are getting better, but this is still my tool of choice.
- **Extremely customizable queries** – Using special syntax (text strings in a specific format), Google allows you to refine your search so much so that you can find every page on cnn.com that mentions Indiana Jones but only if the page also has a link containing the text *harrison ford*. That's a lot of power and flexibility. A bit later on, you'll learn how to harness this power for your own needs.

- **Integration with other Google engines/services** – Google provides so many services that 'do their thing' based on a query (image, video, news search, books etc.). All of these services are top-quality. Fortunately, when using Google to search the Web, you're typically just a click away from feeding/sending your query to any of these other services and benefiting from the results.
- **Universal Search** – Leveraging its own services as previously mentioned, Google uses what is called Universal Search, which in a nutshell displays the most relevant content (not only Web pages, but images, news, books, video, etc.) on the search results page. For example, when you type a query related to something currently popular i.e. Call of Duty Ghosts, in addition to the normal Web results, you'll see listings for related videos and news content. Universal Search results include news headlines, maps, definitions, encyclopedic content, stock info, movie reviews, and more, basically whatever is relevant to the specific search.

Call of Duty: Ghosts - Wikipedia, the free encyclopedia
en.wikipedia.org/wiki/Call_of_Duty:_Ghosts
Call of Duty: Ghosts is a 2013 first-person shooter video game developed by Infinity Ward, with assistance from Raven Software and Neversoft, and published by ...
IW engine - Kinetic bombardment - Stephen Gaghan

News for **call of duty ghosts**

Call of Duty: Ghosts Gets a New Update and Heavy Duty Multiplayer Mode
The Gamer Headlines - 15 hours ago
Infinity Ward has released the new update for **Call of Duty: Ghosts**. With the update, players will now be able to enjoy the new Heavy Duty ...

'**Call of Duty: Ghosts**' Update Adds New Heavy Duty Mode
Game Rant - 13 hours ago

Call of Duty: Ghosts - Tips to master Cranked
Attack of the Fanboy - 23 hours ago

Call of Duty: Ghosts - The Call of Duty Wiki - Wikia
callofduty.wikia.com/wiki/Call_of_Duty:_Ghosts
"Everyone was expecting us to make Modern Warfare 4, which would have been the safe thing to...

Official **Call of Duty: Ghosts** Reveal Trailer - YouTube

www.youtube.com/watch?v=Zxnx3W-HA18
May 21, 2013 - Uploaded by CALLOFDUTY
Call of Duty: Ghosts takes the critically-acclaimed franchise into the next generation. New world. New story ...

Resources:

- https://support.google.com/websearch/
- http://www.google.com/intl/en/help/features.html
  – Special features of Google you should know about!

Bing.com and Yahoo.com

While I do use Yahoo and Bing occasionally, I still prefer Google and I'm a strong advocate of its capabilities as a search engine. In my experience, the search results from Bing/Yahoo are generally similar to Google so I'm not going to spend much time covering their features other than to say that many of the tips and tricks I'm going to share can be applied to these as well. At the end of the day, it's all about finding the information you want and need so by all means use those if you're getting better results.

Clusty.com

While the name of this search engine sounds more like a clown name and you may never have heard of it, it actually does accurately describe its big selling-point as a search engine.

Clustered results – In addition to listing search results in order of relevance, Clusty also organizes them into logical groups (clusters), helping you 'drill down' within the results to help you find exactly what you're looking for:

The cluster panel is on the left side of every search results page, and consists of 4 tabs – clouds, sources, sites and time. Clicking a 'cluster' link will refine your search accordingly. The graphic below shows the various clusters for the query, '*wii u*'.

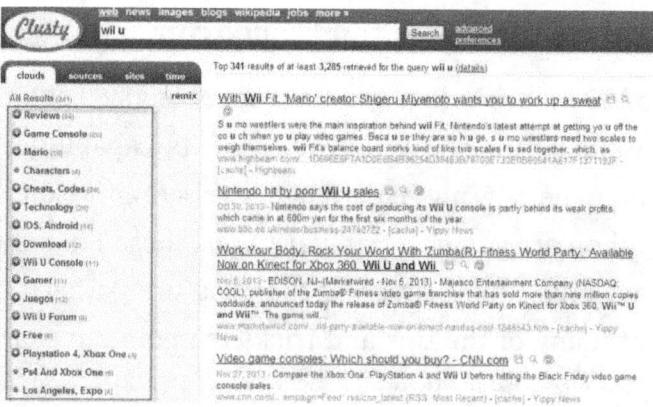

How to Become a Search Ninja

*T*o drive home the importance of expanding your search skills beyond what they probably are now, I'd like to take a minute to perform an interesting experiment using the most powerful computer in the world – your brain.

What can you tell me about the keyword Mustang?
Think real hard, I can wait...
Well? What did you come up with?

Let me see if I can guess. It's an American muscle car made by Ford. They're beautiful, expensive cars, historically built in the US. Steve McQueen drove one in the movie 'Bullitt'.

If that's what you came up with, then good for you. The only problem is I was looking for information about the horse breed that is known as a Mustang.

How is it that such a simple question confused the most powerful computer in the world?

Mainly because Mustang has different meanings depending on context (in my example, it's a car and a horse) but you had no way to know which meaning I wanted information about.

Unfortunately, most people's approach to searching for information is pretty much the same way; they expect to be able to type a simple one or two word query into a search engine and expect the engine to know exactly what they're looking for.

While you can still get good results using this approach, with a few simple search concepts in your arsenal, you can boost the power of those searches into hyper drive.

Add More Keywords to Your Search

May seem obvious to you, but because it's so simple, many people miss it.

Add as many keywords to your search query as it takes to pinpoint exactly what you're looking for – add details and specifics. Search engines are very forgiving as to how much text your query can include, so use as much as you need, even if it's a dozen words.
For example: *ford mustang models from 1967 to 1975*

You might consider entering your query in the form of a statement or question:
How many ford mustangs were made in 1967?

Here's information from the 1st site returned in the results of that search:

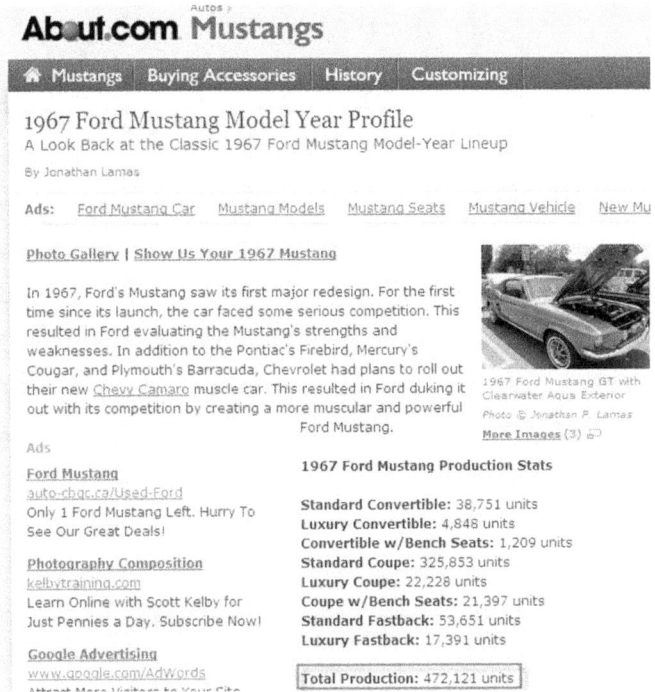

The more details you add to your search query, the more accurate your results will be.

Details are not always easy to come by, so if you need some inspiration, check out the following tools, which will take a general keyword (such as *golf*), and return a list of suggested searches that contain that keyword.

Let the keywords in the list help you in creating a useful search query for your specific needs.

Here are those tools:
- http://www.keyworddiscovery.com/search.html
- http://www.WordTracker.com

Results for the keyword "golf":

Query: golf

Results 1 - 100 of 38689   Page: 1 2 3 4 5 6 7 8 9 10

Search Term	Total ?
golf	26912
golf cart	7178
golf 4	2167
golf-gti	2013
volkswagen golf	1294
golf clubs	1251
golf gti	1245
golf 3	1221
volkswagen-golf	953
vw golf	941
golf carts	844
golf 5	820
golf 2	806
gas golf cart	733
golf 7	578
juegos de golf	520
golf rebaixado	505
golf club	461
golf 6	412
golf 2013	403
golf 4 tdi	394
golf instruction	338
golf-2000	321
golf-2008	318
golf car	298
novo golf 2013	283

Tips/Notes: Some search engines, like Google, Bing and Yahoo, have a suggested keyword feature built-in but is limited in the number of search terms displayed compared to using the tools mentioned previously.

Use of Negative Keywords

A negative keyword is simply a way to tell most search engines (especially Google) what you don't want included in your search results.

The way you define a negative keyword in your query is either by using the term NOT before the keyword, or in some cases (as with Google), simply placing a minus sign (-) before it (see the example below).

As we saw earlier, some words have more than a single meaning, and this is when the use of negative keywords really helps.

For example, when searching for content related to jaguar (the animal), you can achieve a lot more relevant results by telling Google that you're not looking for info related to the car or the Apple operating system by using the following syntax:

jaguar -car -cars -models -apple -os

Be sure when using the minus sign that there isn't a space between it and the negative keyword.

Use Quotes in Your Query

This one may be a no-brainer for some, but it's worth mentioning anyway, especially for those who have never used it.

When you enter a multi-word query into most search engines, it will return pages that contain all of your keywords, no matter where they are on the page, even if they're not right next to each other.

Sometimes that's ok, but most times, finding content related to your query exactly as you entered it is a must. For example, when looking for something with a name (a person, book, song, band, TV show, etc.), you'll want to use quotes ("") around your query.

Another thing to be aware of is that some search engines, like Google, automatically remove some common words (a, the, be, to, is, etc.) from a query unless they are placed within quotes. So if your query contains any of these words, and they are important to what you're looking for, add quotes to it.

Use OR to Speed Up Your Searches

Did you know that *OR* can speed up your web searches?

There are times when you'll find yourself searching for key phrases (queries containing more than a single word) that look similar to one another:

- Blueberry pie
- Apple pie
- Sugar pie (yes there is such a thing and it is delicious)
- Strawberry pie

The similarities of these queries are obvious – they all contain the word *pie*.

Now, you could do a search for *blueberry pie*, look at the results, do another search for *apple pie*, look at the results, and continue on down your list using the 'hard' way of searching, or you could do it the 'smart' way – by adding OR to your query.

Look at this updated query:

blueberry OR apple OR sugar OR strawberry pie

This single query will return results for all your pie needs :-)

Great thing is this tool has many applications other than pie. Here are some other examples:
- *decorating OR diy OR painting tips*
- *halloween costumes OR movies OR decorations*
- *dairy OR deli meat OR produce recalls*

On Google, you can use the *Pipe* symbol (|), which is the uppercase character of the backslash key (\) instead of using OR: *decorating | diy | painting tips*

Ask for Synonym Results

Until I learned this trick, I never thought I would have a need to use the tilde character (~) on my keyboard (the uppercase character to the left of the *1* on your keyboard).

Well, Google has found a clever use for it.

This character can be used in your query to define words where a synonym of the word (a word with a similar meaning) should be searched for and returned in results.

For example, a query of *~dog* returns results related to dog, dogs, pet, pets, puppy, puppies, animal, and others.

A search for *~car* will return results for car, cars, motor, automobile, truck, and even BMW.

Your query can combine synonym-enhanced words with non-synonym-enhanced words:

~dog toys

To my knowledge, this is a Google-only feature.

Why Titles Matter

Every Web page has a feature known as a title that describes the overall content of the page.

When viewing a Web page in your browser, its title is displayed in the upper-left corner of the browser window:

Smart web designers have learned the importance of choosing good, relevant titles for their pages. Why? Well, for one thing, it's just common sense. But another valuable reason is that search engines give a lot of weight to page titles when determining the meaning of the content on that page. The assumption is that the page title most accurately represents the idea or concept that its creator/publisher is trying to convey, no matter what other text, links, or images may be on the page.

When searching Google, you can use this to your advantage in order to find content that is highly relevant to your query. Just tell Google you only want to see pages that include all of your keywords in the page title. You do this by entering your query as like this: *allintitle:how to fix faucet leak*

When I performed this search, Google returned just 1,060 results. I can almost guarantee you that most of these are very relevant pages about how to fix a faucet leak.

Removing *allintitle:* from my query brings me 1,340,000 results. Why the discrepancy? Because now, Google is returning all pages that contain my keywords anywhere on the page – even if the page has little to do with faucet leaks.

This can be one of the most powerful search tricks you can use!

Whether you're looking for tips, news, facts, or FAQs about a topic, using *allintitle:* will likely help you find what you're looking for faster than just about anything else.

There may be times when using this feature on Google brings you few or no results. In that case, you can use *allintitle:*'s relative, *intitle:* to tell Google that not all your keywords need to be in the page title, just specific ones. For example: *intitle:faucet how to fix leak*

Since the word *faucet* immediately follows *intitle:*, you're telling Google that it's the only word in your query that needs to be found in the title of pages returned. The other words can be found anywhere on the page (including but not limited to the page title). By the way this query returned 95,700 results.

Other way of explaining this feature is that you're telling Google to give more weight to specific keywords in your query.

Use *intitle:* directly before any word in your query that you want to be found in a page's title:

intitle:usain intitle:bolt statistics

I think overall *allintitle:* is more powerful, but using *intitle:* can be useful when you still want to maximize the relevancy of the results you get, but you want more results to view.

Reverse Your Keywords

Moving keywords around in a multi-word query usually brings you different, but generally just as relevant results.

For example, *gardening tips* will return a different set of results than *tips gardening*.

Change-up your query keyword order on occasion, and you'll be surprised at the results.

Combine All These Strategies When Searching

That's right, take all the things you've learned about searching, and mash them up to customize your search results like never before.

Look at this query, which combines a number of tricks you've learned so far: *allintitle:~dog "care tips" | training*

Before you picked up this book, you may have looked at this query wondering what in the world it meant. Now you know that it simply tells Google that you're looking for any page that has dog, puppy, canine "care tips" (with those two words next to each other) OR training in the page's title.

Armed with these tricks, I would say you're a better web searcher than 90% of the people out there. But we're just scratching the surface.

Become an Explorer

*T*o unlock gigabytes of relevant content, use discovery keywords. What is a 'discovery' keyword? It's nothing more than a special keyword that, when used in conjunction with most general keywords, can help you quickly find extremely useful/helpful information related to your topic.

Here are some 'discovery' keyword examples:
- tips
- articles
- guide
- checklist
- FAQs
- resources
- information
- help
- facts
- secrets
- how to
- tutorials
- discussion
- resources
- links
- top 10
- ways
- tricks

- manual
- handbook

Fortunately, they are quite simple to use. For example, instead of searching for *'Australia travel'*, search for *'Australia travel tips'*, *'Australia travel articles'*, *'Australia travel guide'*, and so on. Instead of searching for *'buying a car'*, search for *'buying a car tips'*, or *'buying a car guide'*. Just add the discovery keyword to your regular search query.

Try it and you'll be pleasantly surprised at the boost in quality search results you'll get.

Tips/Notes: When using Google, the combination of [your query] information will often bring Wikipedia entries to the top of the search results page.

More Tips That You Can Handle

*W*hat I'm about to share with you is a special 'search trick' that will help you use Google to discover all kinds of tips, hacks, and how to's on practically anything you can imagine.

The reason this is so powerful is that the Internet contains thousands and thousands of pages that provide information like:

- 3 Steps to whatever…
- 20 Steps to whatever…
- 7 Ways to whatever…
- 21 Ways to whatever
- 25 Secrets for whatever…
- 101 Secrets for whatever…
- Or various other combinations

This is something that only a small minority of people know about and actually use and is advanced, but simple to customize for your needs. This is what it looks like:

DIY-related Tips:

allintitle:3 | 5 | 7 | 10 | 20 | 25 | 100 | 101 tips | steps | ways | hacks | secrets -site:amazon.com -site:ebay.com diy

Golf-related Tips:

allintitle:3 | 5 | 7 | 10 | 20 | 25 | 100 | 101 tips | steps | ways | hacks | secrets -site:amazon.com -site:ebay.com golf

Gardening-related Tips:

allintitle:3 | 5 | 7 | 10 | 20 | 25 | 100 | 101 tips | steps | ways | hacks | secrets -site:amazon.com -site:ebay.com gardening

To customize this search, just swap out the keyword at the very end of the query with one relevant for you.

Tips/Notes: This is a long search query and not easy to remember, so once you have it in Google, bookmark the Google results page. To use it later, select that bookmark, return to the Google results page, and edit the keyword/keyphrase in the query according to your needs.

Related Searches

*N*early every person, place, or thing you'll search for has a number of terms related to it, which if you know, will let you to tap into a goldmine of relevant, related information that may be more helpful in your search than you can imagine.

For example, if you're looking for information about New York travel, can you think of any keywords that might help you find information *related* to New York travel?

How about:
- Broadway
- Manhattan
- Times Square
- Central Park
- Madison Square Garden

Would knowing these keywords and searching for information about them help in your overall results for information about New York travel?

Probably.

Or how about another example: Would searching for any of the following related keywords help in your search for information related to 'diet':
- Weight loss
- Low fat recipes
- Fat burning workouts

- Fitness programs

Most likely.

Related keywords can help you expand the scope of your search into many useful areas and as a result lead to great content.

So, how do you come up with keywords that are related to your main search?

Well, the manual way is to try to come up with some on your own which is not always the easiest thing to do.

An easier way is to head over to web tool like http://www.keyworddiscovery.com/search.html and search for your original keyword there.

When you do this, you will see a series of keywords, which are terms related to the term you're searching for.

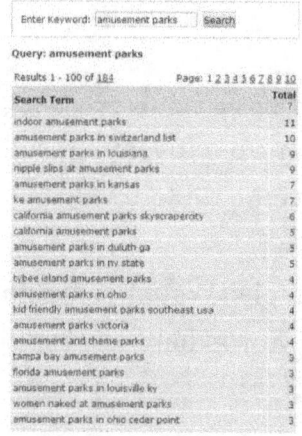 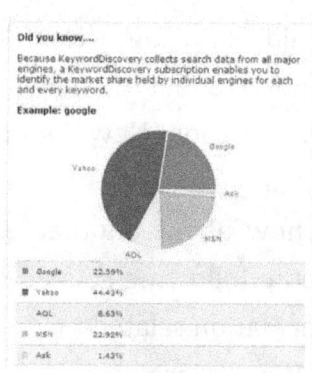

Another approach is to use WikiMindMap.org. By entering your keyword and clicking Search, you'll get a list of branches that you can expand to reveal various related keywords you can use to expand your search results.

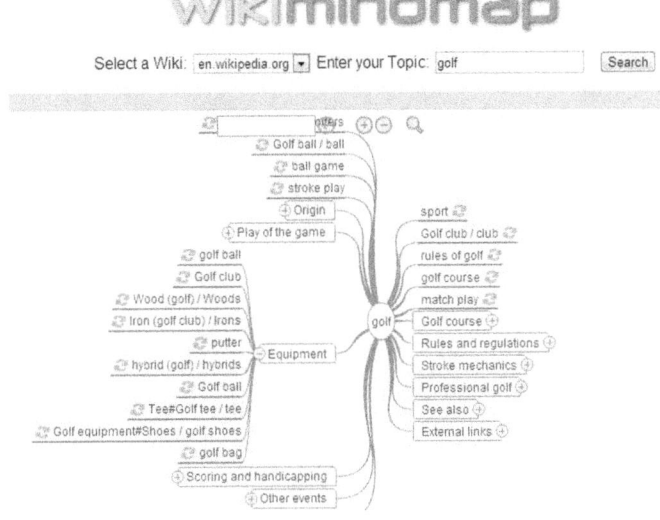

Tips/Notes: Many Search Engines provide lists of Related Keywords somewhere on the results page but is generally less extensive than the Search Term Discovery Tool.

Lightning Speed Results

*I*n some cases, you can dramatically speed up your search results by using search shortcuts. The top search engines (ie. Google, Yahoo, and Bing) all offer search shortcuts. They may call them different things, but they essentially all work the same.

Here's how:

If you want the weather for your City, head over to Google, Yahoo or Bing and enter your location like you see below and you will get exactly what you asked for:

weather Moncton

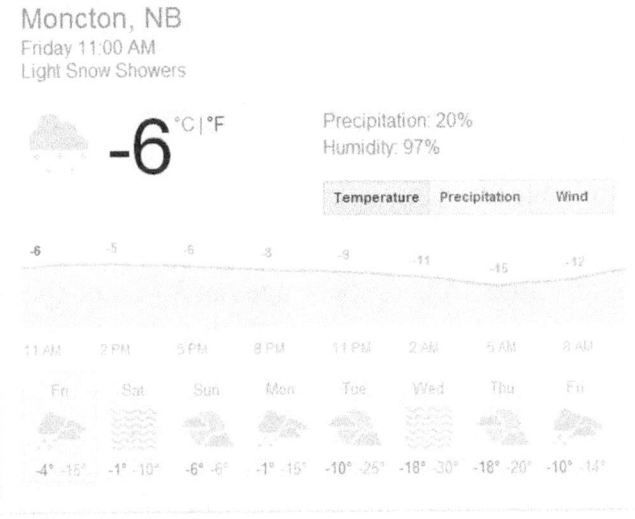

Want a definition for a word? Google, Yahoo, and Ask will all allow you to find it quickly by entering your search the following way: *define sip*

sip
/sip/
verb
1. drink (something) by taking small mouthfuls.
   "I sat sipping coffee"
   synonyms: drink (slowly) More

noun
1. a small mouthful of liquid.
   "she took a sip of the red wine"
   synonyms: mouthful, swallow, drink, drop, dram, nip, taste; More

The addition of the term 'define' to your query tells the search engine you're looking for a definition for the word that follows.

These are just a couple of the dozens of search shortcuts the various search engines provide.

With search shortcuts you can quickly find:
- The weather
- Flight information
- Movie show times
- Scores for a particular sports team
- Exchange rates
- And much more...

Here are links to shortcut pages of some of the search engines. Try these out for yourself. They can be real time-savers.

Resources:
- http://www.google.com/help/features.html
- http://tools.search.yahoo.com/shortcuts/

Google Deep Dive

*B*elieve it or not, there's a site online which shows you how to get the most from Google, and it's better than Google's own help section.

The site is called 'Google Guide'.

http://www.googleguide.com

While what you've learned about searching up to this point will really boost the quality of the results you now get, if you want to dig even deeper into Google specific functionality, this is the place for you.

The site contains great explanations, screenshots and tons of examples.

News that Matters to You

There are a number of great sites that provide news 24/7. Some of the more popular ones include:
- http://news.google.com
- http://news.yahoo.com
- http://www.cbc.ca/news
- http://www.cnn.com
- http://www.msnbc.com
- http://www.bbc.co.uk

These sites provide all of today's news, which quickly changes by the minute.

When looking for news on a specific topic, maybe something that occurred in the past, you need some more search power.

Use Advanced Search

Both Google News Advanced Search and Yahoo News Advanced Search provide useful news search options that allow you to specify exactly what type of news content you're looking for. These options include:
- **A publish date** – To help you locate stories published within the past week only, for example
- **A source** – If you only want stories from CNN, or New York Times
- **A location** – For news stories related to a specific geographical location such as Italy, or California

Typically, when performing an advanced news search, you'll specify either a source or a location, not both.

```
Find news stories that have
all these words:
[                              ]
this exact phrase:
[                              ]
at least one of these words:
[                              ]
none of these words:
[                              ]
occurring  [anywhere in the article ⬍]
Date added:
          [   anytime   ⬍]   Looking for archive content?
                             Learn more
between [M/d/yy]  and  [M/d/yy]
Source:
[E.g. CNN, New York Times        ]
Location:
[E.g. California, India           ]
[Search]
```

Do a Web News Search

While Google News and Yahoo News do a good job of finding specific news articles from multiple sources around the world, there are many sites that provide news in a specific niche that you may be interested in. A simple Web search helps you find these. Simply add *news* to the name of a topic:

- disney news

- hockey news
- photoshop news
- android news
- barack obama news

Use the name of a person, place or thing.

For additional news archives, you may want to explore the following links:
- Links to U.S. news archives (http://www.ibiblio.org/slanews/internet/archives.html)
- Links to international news archives (http://www.ibiblio.org/slanews/internet/intarchives.htm)

Do a Web Search for News Archives

You can go beyond a specific 'news archive' service/site and its limited results/resources, and do a Web search for *news archive*, which will return news archives around the Internet.

In addition, to find specific news archives (such as for space, sailing, entertainment, etc.), do a Google Web search using the topic you're interested in, followed by the keyphrase, *news archive*:
- space news archive
- sailing news archive
- entertainment news archive

Tips/Notes: Are you sick of the constant flow of bad news from mainstream media? If you're interested in positive, inspirational news stories, check out http://www.happynews.com.

Go Treasure Hunting

You may not realize it, but there are literally millions of documents, spreadsheets, presentations, and other files online. Things such as manuals, ebooks, guides, reports and how to's.

Based on my experience, a Web search will usually produce the best results for most queries, but sometimes a specific search for a PDF (ebook) or a PowerPoint presentation has helped me find some extremely useful documents/files/resources.

Use Google to Discover Files

Using Google to find files that may be of interest to you is pretty easy. You just need to tell Google what type of file you're looking for when doing your search. You do this by adding a little bit of text to your query that looks like this: *filetype:[file extension]*

Replace *[file extension]* with any of the following (make sure there isn't a space between the colon (:) and the file extension):

- **pdf** – For ebooks/PDF documents
- **doc** – For Microsoft Word documents (docx for newer versions)
- **xls** – For Microsoft Excel spreadsheets (xlsx for newer versions)

- **ppt** – For Microsoft PowerPoint presentations (pptx for new versions)

So to find a PDF/ebook about golf tips, what you type into Google's search box would look like this:
golf tips filetype:pdf

This kind of search will return PDFs that contain 'golf tips' anywhere within the document.

As with most searches on Google, you'll get even more relevant results by using *allintitle:* in your query, as shown here: *allintitle:golf tips filetype:pdf*

Use this kind of search to discover:
- children's books (*[name of book] filetype:pdf*)
- tax forms (*[name of form] filetype:pdf*)
- product brochures (*[name of product/model number] filetype:pdf*)
- travel brochures (*[name of location] filetype:pdf*)
- application forms (*[type of application] filetype:pdf*)
- various other forms, like legal, real estate, etc. (*[name of form] filetype:pdf*)

Use Yahoo to Discover Files

While Google is great at finding files, it's not the only option. Having choices when doing any search is a good thing.

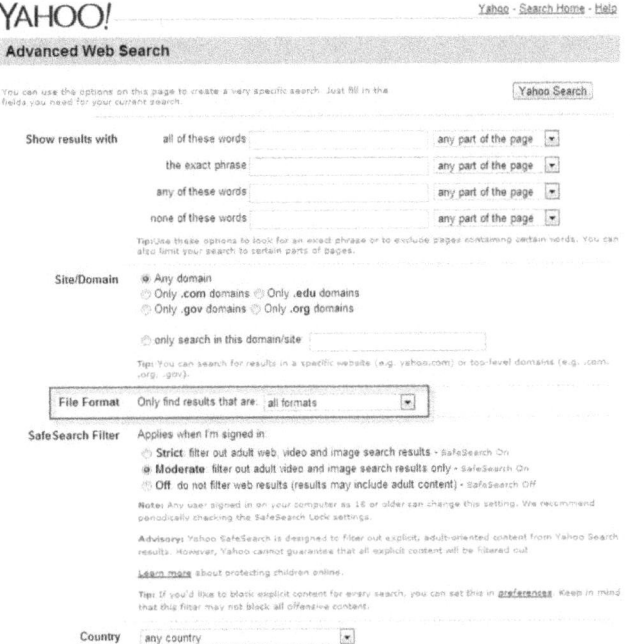

With that in mind, let's look at how to find files using Yahoo. In order to find specific file types, Yahoo provides an advanced search form as seen above.

All you need to do is type your keyword and select the File Format you want. You have access to the same file extensions as Google.

Site Search Secrets

Although the Internet as a whole is a great content resource, chances are you have a number of favorite sites that you visit regularly because they have information that interests you, whether your interest is pottery or fitness.

It's time to learn how to mine every last nugget of useful information out of one of your favorite sites and turn it into your personal content resource.

Use Google to Find Specific Content on Any Site

A lot of sites these days have their own search box, but some don't, and even those that do, may not do that great of a job. Not a problem, because Google has a cool feature that allows you to customize your search so that the results that come back are only from the Website you specify.

To use this feature of Google, enter something like the following into Google's main search box:

hockey site:cbc.ca

As you can probably tell, you're just telling Google to return pages about hockey from cbc.ca, *only*.

If you want to only see pages on cbc.ca that use the term *hockey* in the title of the page, you would enter this:

allintitle:hockey site:cbc.ca

Basically, you'll want to replace the keyword(s) and site url in the example with yours.

Extract the Images from Any Site

Depending on the topic, there are some sites on the Web (especially travel-related sites) that contain tons of wonderful images. Unfortunately, to view them, you usually find yourself having to navigate menus, etc.

With this trick, you'll be able to use Google Images and/or Yahoo Images to extract and display a site's images in a format that's much easier to view and navigate.

All you need to do to take advantage of this image search functionality is to visit either Google Images or Yahoo Images and enter *site:* into the main search box, followed by the domain name of the site you want images from.

For example: *site:hawaiipictures.com*

This will display all the photos Google Images has found at hawaiipictures.com.

Want to filter your results even more, add a keyword to your search in the following way:

rainbow site:hawaiipictures.com

Do this with some of your favorite sites, and you'll be surprised at some of the things you'll find.

Extract Files from a Site

It's very common for sites to contain files such as ebooks, special reports, white papers, and electronic brochures. Sometime it's easy to find them, sometimes it's not. Again – not a problem.

I've been absolutely blown away at some of the great stuff I've been able to find over the years using the trick I'm about to show you.

If you know of a site that might contain ebooks, reports, and similar documents, use the following search on Google to find them quickly and easily:

site:ebay.com filetype:pdf

With this search, I'm telling Google to show me any PDF documents it finds on Ebay.

You'll find that the following types of sites contain a wealth of content like this:

- universities/schools
- government sites
- travel-related sites
- commercial/corporate sites
- news site

Of course, in addition to PDF files, you can discover Word documents, Excel spreadsheets, and PowerPoint presentations on sites in the same way. Just replace *pdf* in the search with *doc, xls,* or *ppt*, respectively (To find newer versions of MS Office documents, use *xlsx, docx, pptx*).

Discover Related Sites

Have you ever found a great site and wanted to find more just like it? This is where Alexa.com's Related Sites feature is very helpful.

By entering the following URL into your browser's address bar (replacing the example site URL of *bhg.com* with your own):

http://www.alexa.com/data/details/related_links?url=bhg.com

If you scroll down a bit, Alexa provides you a list of sites related to the one you specified:

What sites are related to bhg.com?

Related Links

1. marthastewart.com
2. lhj.com
3. magazines.ivillage.com
4. goodhousekeeping.com
5. familycircle.com

More

Other Sites Owned

1. agriculture.com
2. americanbaby.com
3. betterrecipes.com
4. bhg.com
5. bhgscrapbooksetc.com

More

This can be a very useful way of finding sites with related content that you can use to expand your knowledge.

I Want Answers!

*I*n day to day life we naturally have questions about different things and lucky for us there are a lot of people out there willing to answer them. You can let the collective knowledge of your peers help you by posting your question(s) on one of the many answer sites online. Here's a listing of some of the best 'Answer' sites:

Submit Your Question on Yahoo Answers

Yahoo Answers is a popular community site for people to ask and answer questions – questions about anything and everything. Here's a sampling of a few current questions:

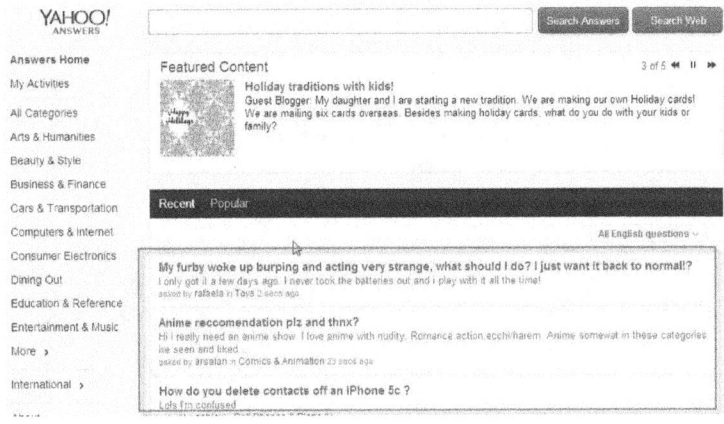

The process is simple. Sign up for a Yahoo account and then enter your question in the box.

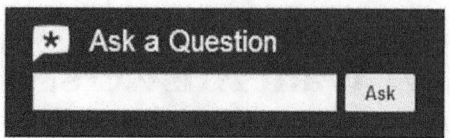

Resources: http://answers.yahoo.com/info/welcome

Submit Your Question on Amazon's AskVille

Askville is service that Amazon.com launched to compete with Yahoo Answers.

While the core concept between the sites is the same – people ask questions, other people provide answers – Askville provides a different set of tools for answering questions.

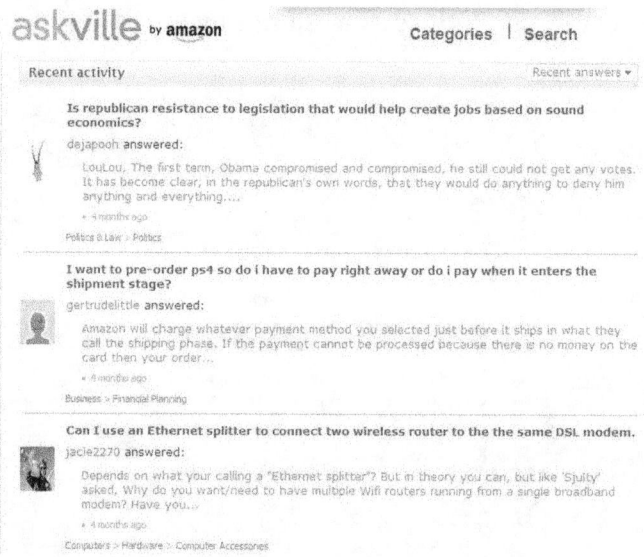

Resources: http://askville.amazon.com/faq.html

Post Your Question on Wiki.Answers.com

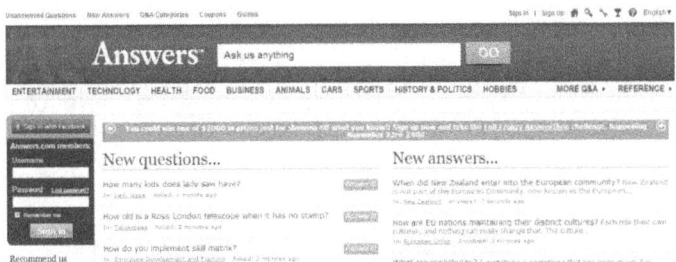

Another online community willing to help answer your every question can be found at wiki.answers.com.

According to the site it has 225 million registered users.

Post Your Question on Answerbag.com

Along the same lines as wiki.answers.com is Answerbag.com.

Want a list of questions related to the topic you want answers for (tennis, herbal remedies, etc.)? Click on the Questions tab at the top of the page. This may provide answers to questions you didn't even realize you wanted answers to.

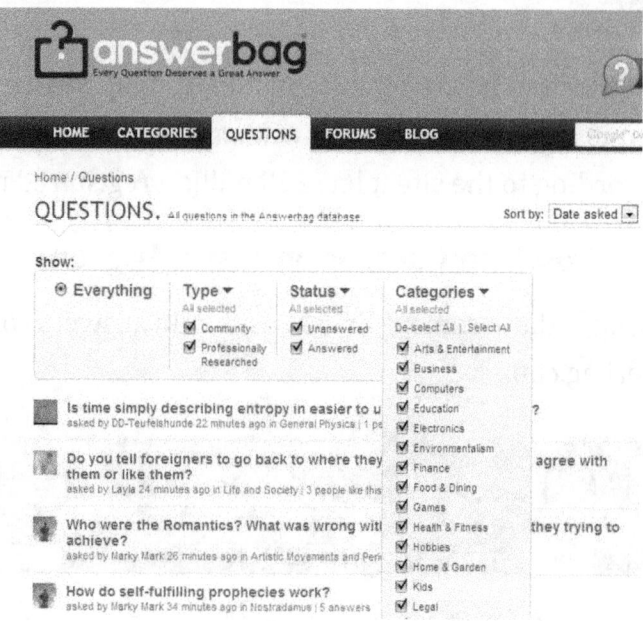

Another nice feature of Answerbag is that its various categories are RSS-enabled, meaning you can subscribe to individual categories of questions and answers. Look for the RSS feed at the top right of most pages.

Ask.com

What I like about Ask.com is that it's a hybrid between a search engine and an Answer site. For example, if I type in "how do I start running", I'll get related ads, popular answers and related Questions but can also drill down based on category.

In my running question example above, I could quickly find related videos, apps or books by clicking the appropriate category in the left of the screen.

Tips/Notes:
- Be aware that any information you receive from any online source may not be completely accurate. Be sure to check your facts (maybe using a secondary source) if the answer is really important.

- Be cautious on these sites. Some topics/responses may be real eye*openers for you, as anonymity on the Internet tends to cause some people to throw most of their inhibitions aka common sense out the window.
- Expect that at some point, some people will provide answers with a dose or sarcasm or plain rudeness. Some people and I use that word loosely stoop so low as to personally attack your intelligence. Don't take it personally, just move on.

Crowdsourced Encyclopedia

In case you haven't heard, Wikipedia.org is an online encyclopedia that has marched its way to the top of the Web to become the most popular source for encyclopedic information on the planet.

If you're looking for information about anything – and I do mean anything – chances are that you'll find more than you could ever imagine on Wikipedia.

Content on Wikipedia is also available in a number of languages.

What makes Wikipedia so great?

- **Collective knowledge** – Wikipedia (and you) benefits from the collective knowledge of everyone who wants to join in and contribute – and a lot of people do.
- **Exhaustive** – It's amazing what you can discover on Wikipedia. From obscure places, to obscure people, chances are, you'll find something about it on Wikipedia.
- **Ad free** – Incredibly, Wikipedia is ad-free which does something to enhance the user experience.
- **Join in** – Add your own uniqueness to Wikipedia.

Tips/Notes:

- Because Wikipedia can be edited by practically anyone, the accuracy of some of its content has been called into question by various media sources so as with most information Online, use it at your own discretion.
- Additional services available by those Wiki folks include:Wiktionary.org (dictionary), Wikiquotes.org, species.wikimedia.org, and Wikibooks.org (public domain books).
- WikiMindMap.org is a site that allows you to view Wikipedia articles about a topic in the form of a mind map, which is an interesting way to visualize how various aspects of a topic fit together.

'How To' Nirvana

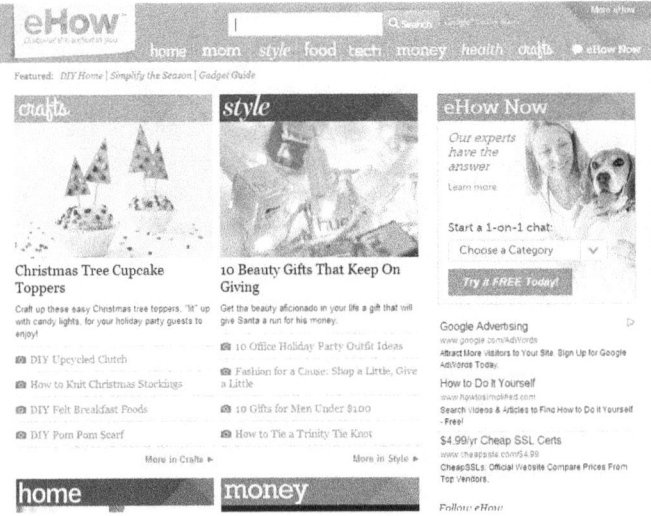

*T*his site is a genuine 'how to' paradise. In fact, after just a short time on the site, you may realize, like I did, that you're not half as smart as you thought you were.

eHow.com is all about helping you do every day stuff better:

- 5 ways to save at a drug store
- How to change a tire
- How to melt caramel squares
- Build your own firewood rack

Like many sites these days, eHow is all about community. If you have a how-to you want to share with the world, eHow wants it. Or if you'd like to add some content to an existing how-to, you can do that too.

Content Powerhouse

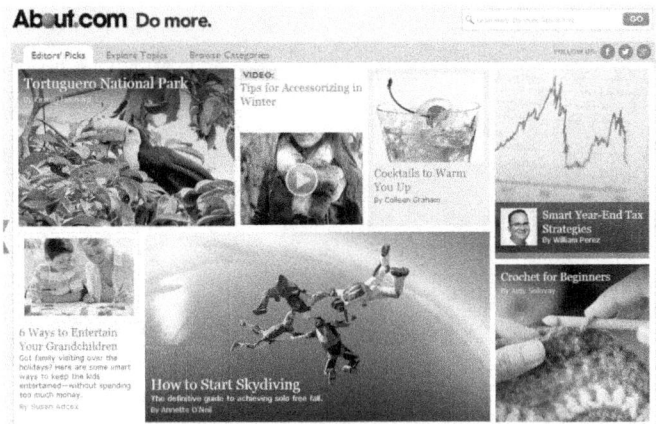

About.com is a content powerhouse and a popular online destination with approximately 25% of the U.S. visiting each month. They focus on providing high-quality information on almost every topic, ranging from cooking to parenting to healthcare and travel. Content is provided by a group of nearly 1,000 contributors who are people with a real passion for the topic and demonstrated expertise in their fields.

Discover rich content 'guides' on practically any topic you can imagine plus there's a growing library of video content, on everything from auto tips/advice to software tutorials.

How Does That Work?

*H*owStuffWorks.com is actually a very extensive site for those who like to ask the question, 'how?'

You'll find out how all kinds of cool and interesting stuff works in the world around you.

Of course, if you'd rather watch than read about how stuff works, you can do that by visiting the site's video directory.

Fine-Tune Your Life

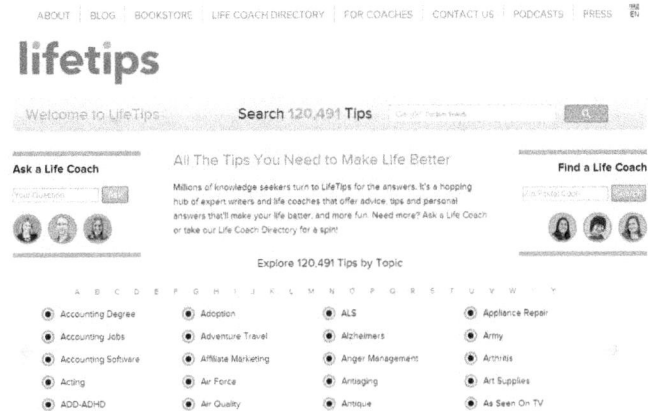

*E*very now and then, life needs a bit of 'fine-tuning'. To help make the fine-tuning process as simple as possible, there's Lifetips.com.

As of this writing, Lifetips.com contains 120,491 tips to help you do everything from parenting your adopted child to choosing a cell phone plan.

Life Hacks

Lifehacker.com is a continuously updated site that provides a never ending supply of tips, advice, and downloads on how to get more done in life using 21st century tools and gadgets.

While it can be tech heavy at times, there is usually something for everyone that pops up regularly.

Bargains from Misspellings

*I*f you've ever used eBay, you know that the more people who want an item that's for sale, the higher the bid price will be. That's what makes auctions such a great selling tool.

People typically find items they want by doing a search on eBay – search for *disney*, you'll find disney related products.

An interesting thing happens with the thousands of new auctions started every day. A number of sellers list items incorrectly because of spelling errors for whatever reason. As a result, if they create an auction listing for a *disny* related item they want to sell (misspelled on purpose), chances are nobody is searching for *disny* so they will not find it.

This creates an auction with little to no competition which is good for us.

The challenge is how do you find these kinds of auctions? Well, some smart folks have put together a couple of tools for this very purpose.

The first tool, TypoHound.com, sniffs out spelling-challenged auctions on eBay. Enter a correctly spelled keyword, choose the eBay property you want to search (U.S., U.K., Australia, etc.), click the Sniff! button and TypoHound will generate a link for an eBay search. Click the link and prepare to be amazed:

The next tool that helps you find eBay auctions containing misspellings is called FatFingers.co.uk. This site works basically the same way TypoHound does, with a couple of advantages:

- There's an advanced search page where you can create a more precise search
- They offer an app, that allow you to quickly find misspelled auctions without having to navigate to the FatFingers Web site first

Tips/Notes: Use keywords that represent product names (ipod, xbox, etc.), company names (apple, disney, etc.), and product types (headphones, diamond, etc.) when searching for misspelled auctions.

Amazon Unadvertised Deals

*L*ike any store, Amazon.com continually has items that they just want to clear out, and like most stores, the best way of selling it is to lower the price.

Unlike most stores, I've seen discounts of up to 90% off on clothing, electronics, housewares, and more on Amazon.com.

So, where are all these great deals? Well, Amazon doesn't always make it obvious so if you go to Amazon.com/Deals/ you'll find all kinds of savings and discounts.

From this page, you'll be able to access the following deals sections:
- Today's Deals
- Gold Box deals
- Year End Deals
- All Deals
- Coupons
- Outlet
- Deals & Bargains
- Warehouse Deals
- Digital Deals

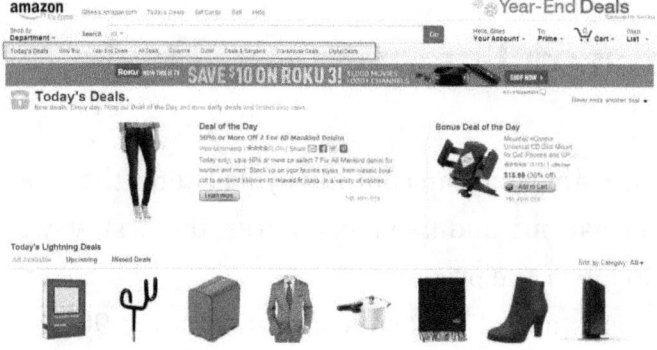

Another way is to use these searches to help you find them:
- Amazon deals
- Amazon discounts
- Amazon deal of the day
- Amazon outlet

Resources:

- How to search for Amazon deals - http://www.brand-name-coupons.com/how-to-search-amazon-for-deals/
- User submitted deals - http://www.reddit.com/r/amazondeals

Buy Gifts Based on Personality

*H*ere's the scenario: You need to buy a gift for your sister, but you have no idea what she might want.

http://www.gifts.com/finder has taken a very unique approach to gift shopping by categorizing products based on the characteristics of the gift receiver. Is the person receiving the gift a woman over 30, someone who is artistic, likes to soak up the sun? Is she career driven or family first, are her favorite shoes stilettos or hiking boots? You get the idea.

Gifts.com has a cool Personality Profiler that will make the job easier.

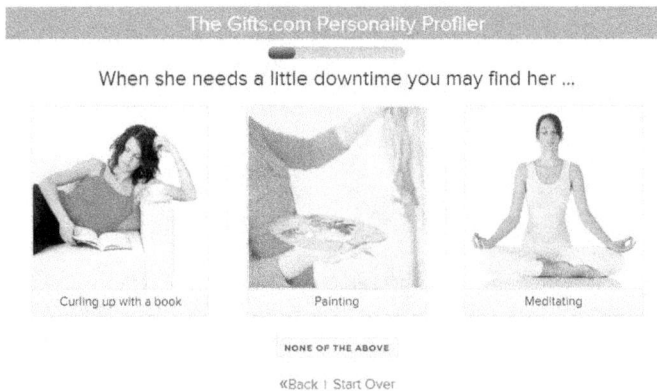

Shop the World

*I*n the real world, shopping can be a real time waster.

Online, it can be much easier: With the right tool, you simply enter what you want to buy into a search box then click a button. Within seconds you can shop stores all around the world. And if that's not good enough, you can quickly filter out items that cost more than you're willing to spend or even those with poor reviews.

Here are three great services for shopping multiple stores in a single shot:

- **Google.com/shopping** – Once again, Google makes the list with their Google Shopping Service. Use it to shop for everything from BBQ sauce to an antique cast iron meat press.
- **TheFind.com** – According to this site's About Us page, it offers over 500 million products from more than 500,000 stores around the world.
- **ShopWiki.com** – This site provides a shopping search engine that brings you over 162,000 stores and 244,000,000 products for your online shopping needs.

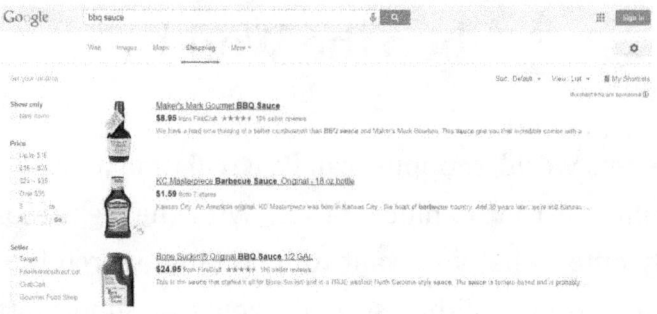

Resources: It would be impossible to list all the great shopping sites online, so here's a great list of the Top 20 comparison shopping sites in case you feel a shopping spree coming on http://www.ebizmba.com/articles/comparison-shopping.html

Save Some Headaches

*S*o far we've looked at how to find great deals, now let's look at what you should *do* before you spend your hard-earned money on anything – be informed!

Ads of any kind (print, web or TV) and talking to a store sales clerk whose job depends on selling products are the absolute worst ways to get unbiased opinions/information about anything you're looking to purchase.

A better way of getting information about products, is to see what real people are saying about them online. A few simple searches are all that's needed.

General searches, which will help you locate what's being said about products, include:
- reviews
- complaints
- recalls

Product category searches include:
- digital camera reviews
- new car reviews
- video game reviews

Product-specific searches include:
- lipton tea reviews
- 2014 toyota camry reviews
- iphone reviews

Use these sample searches as a starting point for your own product research.

Tips/Notes:
- A great resource for reviews includes some of the video-sharing sites like YouTube. Before you buy something, go to one of these sites and enter the name of the product you want to buy. You'll likely find someone or even a professional business that has created a video sharing their thoughts on the product. For greater search accuracy, you may want to add 'review' to your query (2014 toyota camry review).
- As with everything else online, consider the source of the review. Some reviews are disguised sales pitches by people who get a commission if you buy it through their link.

Resources:
- Recalls.gov – U.S. recall information on food, medicine, cars, and other consumer products
- Health Canada: Canadian recall information on food, consumer products, vehicles, health products(Search *Health Canada*)
- Consumer.gov – Your resource for free consumer information from the government
- Office of Consumer Affairs: Canadian resource for free consumer information from the government (Search *Office of Consumer Affairs*)

Product Support Made Easy

*Y*ou've got your shiny new whatever, but what can you do with it, and what do you do if it stops doing what it's supposed to do? You go to the Internet, right!

Here are some strategies to help you get the most from the things you buy.

First, some searches. Let's say I just bought an iPod and I want to learn everything I can about it, I would try the following searches:
- ipod tips
- ipod tricks
- ipod how to
- ipod support
- ipod forum
- ipod discussion

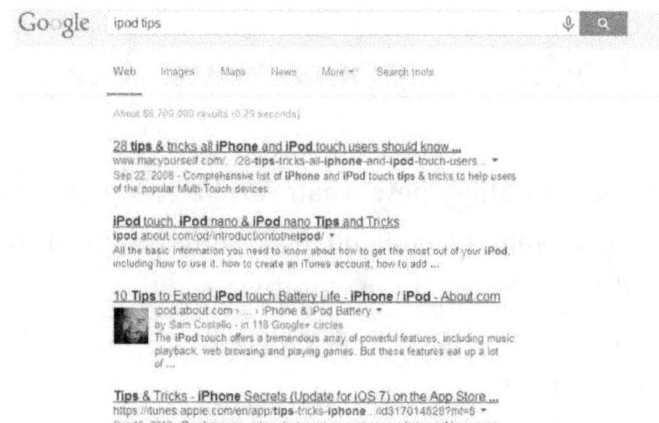

Resources:

- FixYa.com – If you have an issue with one of over 18 million products, this site can help.
- Youtube.com – Believe it or not, if you enter the name or model number of your item into Youtube, you can often find some great video content that may be useful.

How to Replace Books

Why buy a book when you can find the same content online for free?

Here's a simple strategy that could save you a ton of money if you use it.

Review the TOC of a book (especially how to books) either at a bookstore or online using Amazon.com's "Look Inside" feature.

Make a list of topics discussed in the book that interest you. After all, most table of contents' look like nothing more than a list of searches.

Go to Google and do a search for those topics to find a treasure trove of articles, tips, videos, and more, all related to that very topic.

Here's an example of using this strategy with the book, *Personal Finance For Dummies*.

A list of topics the book discusses include:
- setting financial goals
- save more spend less
- saving for big purchases
- taking out car loans (car loan tips)
- dealing with credit mistakes

How to Replace Magazines

*R*eady to save some money on magazines?

Find online versions of a magazine by searching for the name of the magazine:

Examples:
- popular science
- taste of home
- good housekeeping
- readers digest
- national geographic

Find related online content:
- Do a search for [topic/niche] magazine
- Do a search for [topic/niche] news
- Do a search for [topic/niche] blog
- Do a search for [topic/niche] articles

Examples:
- photography magazine
- golf news
- scrapbooking blog
- success articles

Find free online content related to those attention-grabbing headlines:

Examples:
- 10 ways to lose weight for summer
- 20 ways to improve your life
- 7 steps to financial freedom

Use Google Books (http://books.google.com) search to find and view back issues of magazines. Example: *Popular Science*

How to Become a Power Shopper

*T*he Web is a shopper's dream!

Not only does technology help you find the absolute best price for a product, but it gives you access to peoples' real-world experience with a product, so you can avoid buying junk.

Product Categories

To find the best in a product category (TV, juicer, headphones, etc.), just use something similar to the following searches:

- best | top lawn mowers
- lawn mower reviews

Or, simply do a search for the product category (such as lawn mowers) using Google Shopping search, and sort the results by Seller rating.

These days, there are outlet stores, both online and locally that can provide you with deals and discounts on specific product categories, such as shoes, coffee makers, electronics – you name it!

To find them, just use a search like this:

- shoe outlet
- nike outlet

Researching Specific Products

Google Shopping search is also one of the best resources for finding the best price and user reviews for a particular product.

Just do a search for the product name and model number (such as, dyson dc25), and sort by Seller rating to learn other peoples' feelings about the product, and then sort by price to find the best price.

You can also do a regular Google search using the product name and model number, followed by the term, review: *dyson dc25 review*

Find Free, Cheap & Discounted Stuff

Who doesn't like FREE, or even just cheap and discounted?

If you love finding bargains and saving money, here are some ways to use Google to discover enough of them to keep you busy for a very long time.

General Resources for Free & Discounted Stuff

Let's start out finding sites that are all about pointing you to free and discounted stuff. Start with these simple searches:

- freebies
- free stuff
- free samples
- coupons

- coupon | discount | promotional codes
- deals | bargains

Finding Specific Freebies & Discounts

Looking to save money on something in particular (coffee, toothpaste, Tylenol)?

These searches will help:
- free [thing]
- [free [thing] sample
- [thing] coupon

Examples:

- free coffee
- coffee free sample
- coffee coupon
- free toothpaste
- free toothpaste samples
- toothpaste coupon
- Starbucks coupon

Need some inspiration?
- free [a-z]
- free [a-z] sample
- [a-z] coupon

Discount Codes

For other products (usually non-household products), the terminology for finding a discount is a little different – the term 'discount codes' is usually used:
- Avis discount codes
- HP discount codes
- Best Buy discount codes
- vitamin discount codes

Need some inspiration?
- [a-z] discount codes

Search 500,000+ coupons including discount codes from over 50,000 stores at RetailMeNot.com. Discover discounts from popular online as well as brick and mortar stores that include brand name products.

Video Search Power

*W*ith the explosion of online video these days, there are so many things to see beyond music videos, home videos, and blooper reels.

Here's a list of example video searches to get you started:

- **How To's** - how to apply pinstripes, how to dance salsa, how to use photoshop
- **Tips** - camping tips, wedding tips, dog training tips
- **Cartoons** - the flintstones, yogi bear, donald duck cartoon
- **Commercials** - super bowl commercial, classic commercials
- **TV Shows** - andy griffith show, twilight zone, seinfeld
- **Movies** - pirates of the caribbean, pirates of the caribbean theme
- **Videos Games** - just dance 2014 wii, call of duty ghosts
- **Documentaries** - bbc documentary, national geographic documentary
- **Interviews** - president interview, tom hanks interview, rob ford interview
- **Historical Events** - moon landing, chernobyl, beatles arrive in america

- **Historical Figures** - albert einstein, john f kennedy, princess diana
- **Years** - 1943, 1981, 1998
- **Travel** - london travel, las vegas travel
- **Attractions** – Eiffel tower, old faithful, great wall of china
- **Airports** - pearson airport, new delhi airport, orlando airport
- **Drives** - driving in new zealand, driving in europe
- **Tours** - hershey factory tour, tour of venice, tour of white house
- **Recipes** - cake recipe, pizza recipe, salsa recipe
- **Celebrities** - bob hope, johnny depp, oprah
- **Authors/Speakers** - anthony robbins, seth godin, tim ferriss
- **Pets** - labrador, labrador puppies, labrador training, labrador tricks
- **Product/Reviews** - jetta review, vita-mix review
- **Adjectives** - inspiration, amazing, cute, hilarious
- **Slow Motion** - slow motion bullet, slow motion animals
- **Timelapse** - flower time lapse, panama canal time lapse, time lapse painting
- **How It's Made** - how guitars are made, how tires are made, how paper is made
- **Science** - science of flight, science of gravity, science of sleep
- **Mysteries** - bigfoot, loch ness monster, roswell

Image Search Power

*I*mages searches are good for more than just finding photos of people and places. You can use Google Image search to find anything of a visual nature, from documents and cartoons, to plans, posters, and more.

Here's a list of example image searches to try:

- **Documents** - titanic documents, resignation letter, us constitution
- **Covers Of Magazines** - life magazine cover, popular science magazine cover
- **Maps** - old map, london attraction map, new york subway map
- **Sketches** - superman sketch, sketch of a girl, sketch of a face, sketch of a house
- **Art** - watercolor, oil painting, charcoal drawing
- **Artists** - da vinci, picasso, van gogh
- **Nature** - sunset, winter, waterfall
- **Photography** - macro photography, hdr, barn black and white
- **Wallpapers** - nature wallpapers, space wallpaper, australia wallpaper
- **Screenshots** - windows 8 screenshot, office 2010 screenshot
- **Plans** - house plans, dog house plans, landscape design

- **Cutaways** - cutaway, ship cutaway, camera cutaway
- **Attractions** - neuschwanstein castle, abandoned amusement parks
- **Signs** - signs, traffic signs, funny signs, hand signs
- **Adjectives** - funny, crazy, beautiful, amazing
- **Comics** - far side comic, blondie comic, calvin and hobbes comic
- **Movie Posters** - star wars movie poster, indiana jones movie poster
- **Recipes** - onion soup, chocolate truffle cake, enchiladas
- **Cheat Sheets** - cheat sheet, poker cheat sheet, photoshop cheat sheet
- **Checklists** - wedding checklist, moving checklist, travel checklist
- **Infographics** - infographic, history infographic, spending infographic
- **Mind Maps** - mind map, happiness mind map, home business min map
- **Flowcharts** - flowchart, website flowchart, blogging flowchart, funny flowchart
- **Timelines** - timeline, history timeline, titanic timeline
- **Coloring Pages** - mickey mouse coloring pages, spiderman coloring pages
- **Instructions** - origami instructions, baby instructions, tie a tie instructions
- **Puzzles** - crossword puzzles, sudoku, maze

- **Seating Charts** – bell centre seating chart, royal albert hall seating chart
- **Business Cards** - unique business card, funny business card
- **Logos** - olympics logo, mcdonalds logo, denver broncos logo
- **Clipart** - dog clipart, building clipart, animal clipart
- **Chord Charts** - guitar chord chart, piano chord chart, banjo chord chart

Map Search Power

Google Maps not only allows you to virtually travel and discover interesting places all around the world, but if you're planning to visit, you can use it to 'get your bearings' before you go – to see how to get in, get around, and get out.

Here's a list of example map searches to try:
- **Monuments/Landmarks/Attractions** - mount rushmore, taj mahal, red square
- **Parks** – yellowstone national park, fundy national park, fundy trail parkway
- **Theme Parks** – disney world, busch gardens tampa, canada's wonderland
- **Hotels** – chateau frontenac quebec, royal hawaiian hotel
- **Restaurants** – garde manger montreal, hard rock cafe orlando
- **Campuses** - mcgill university, harvard university, hamburg university
- **Stadiums/Arenas/Race Tracks** - daytona international speedway
- **Airports** – pearson international, orlando international airport

Replace Paid Software

As you're probably aware, software can be expensive. Some programs cost hundreds of dollars so if you want to explore free alternatives, then this strategy will help.

Search Google using the following queries in order to find online software applications that replace software you download, install, and sometimes pay for.

- online | free word processor
- online | free spreadsheet
- online | free presentation
- online | free database
- online | free project management
- online | free flowchart
- online | free calendar
- online | free email
- online | free image editor
- online | free photo editor
- online | free photo organizer
- online | free slideshows
- online | free vector editor
- online | free video editor
- online | free screen capture
- online | free sound | audio editor
- online | free html editor
- online | free color picker
- online | free website creator

- online | free organizer
- online | free to do list
- online | free mind mapping
- online | free checkbook
- online | free money manager
- online | free backup
- online | free software
- online | free web conferencing

Time Savers

*T*here's a wealth of valuable information sheets available to you online for free that can save you a tremendous amount of time and frustration. Here's how to find them:

Checklists

To discover checklist resources:
- checklists - Images

To discover specific checklists:
- moving checklist - Images
- wedding checklist - Images

Need inspiration?
- [a-z] checklist - Images
- checklist [a-z] - Images

Forms

To discover form resources:
- free forms

To discover specific forms:
- free real estate forms
- free tax forms
- free legal forms
- free contract forms

Need inspiration?
- free [a-z] forms

Templates

To discover template resources:
- free templates

To discover specific templates:
- free resume template
- free website template
- free powerpoint template
- free invoice template
- free business plan template

Need inspiration?
- free [a-z] template
- free template for [a-z]

Cheat Sheets

To discover cheat sheet resources:
- cheat sheets - Images

To discover specific cheat sheets:
- math cheat sheet – Images
- html cheat sheet - Images

Need inspiration?
- [a-z] cheat sheet – Images

Wildcard

*T*hink of a question you may have about something. For example, "how long do parrots live?". If someone were to answer that question, they might say, "parrots live __ years", where the blank is the answer to the question.

Notice the structure of the answer, because this provides a clue as to how to use the wildcard (*) operator in your searches.

To get the answer to the question using Google, you would enter a search that sounds like an answer, and place the * operator where the answer should appear: *Parrots live * years*

When you run this search, chances are that you'll see the answer to the question highlighted somewhere on the results page.

Animal Care - FOWAS - Friends of the Watsonville Animal Shelter
www.fowas.org/Care_small.html
Finches live 5-10 years, canaries 10-15 years, and many **parrots live 80 years.** They should be given a safe home where they can live out their lives in good ...

How to Decide if a Parrot Is Right for You: 17 Steps - wikiHow
www.wikihow.com › ... › Categories › Pets and Animals › Birds › Parrots
Some **parrots live to be 80 years old**. This is a pet you should leave to someone in your will. Illness, disease, accident, and genetic defect are all things that can ...

Living and Learning with Parrots - by Ginny - YouTube

www.youtube.com/watch?v=_6o6IRalPz0
Jul 17, 2013 - Uploaded by katieslider
Some **parrots live to be 80 years old**. The downside is that they go thru several homes or sanctuaries and ...

To Adopt a Congo African Grey Parrot - Hero Network
heronetwork.com/wish?id=1158523
Mar 7, 2012 - You know **parrots live 50-60 years?** They are very fragile. Air fresheners, fumes and flakes from Teflon frying pans, cleaning products, paint ...

Other examples:

chocolate contains *
vitamin d is good for *
world's tallest office building is * feet tall

Resources

To access the web search resources mentioned in this book, go to http://www.finditnowguide.com/resources/

About the Author

Gilles Côté is an information junkie, data wrangler and search expert who has a passion for exploring the vast resources the Internet holds and loves discovering the 'hidden'nuggets of information that can help him and his family in every facet of daily living.

Having been online since the very early beginnings of the Internet, he's familiar with a lot of online search resources, what they can do, and the various tips and techniques that can be used to extract every last piece of useful content from the Web.

Have feedback, questions or a search tip you want to share? Email me at <u>contact@finditnowguide.com</u>

You can also connect with me online through LinkedIn.com.

www.ingramcontent.com/pod-product-compliance
Lightning Source LLC
Chambersburg PA
CBHW051731170526
45167CB00002B/891